CONNECTED TO CHRIST

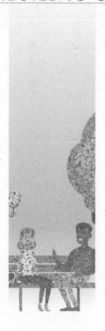

CONNECTED TO CHRIST

Witnessing in Everyday Life

MARK A. WOOD

CONCORDIA PUBLISHING HOUSE • SAINT LOUIS

Published by Concordia Publishing House
3558 S. Jefferson Avenue, St. Louis, MO 63118-3968
1-800-325-3040 · cph.org

Library of Congress Cataloging-in-Publication Data

Names: Wood, Mark A. (Minister), author.

Title: Connected to Christ : witnessing in everyday life / Mark A. Wood.

Description: Saint Louis, MO : Concordia Publishing House, [2021] |

Summary: "Lutheran church members often think of evangelism as a skill they must perfect before witnessing to others. But we are already witnessing of Christ, and we evangelize to those around us every day. Connected to Christ: Everyday Evangelism will provide a Lutheran understanding of a Gospel motivation for sharing God's Word in daily life as well as practical advice for how to do so"-- Provided by publisher.

Identifiers: LCCN 2020050532 (print) | LCCN 2020050533 (ebook) |
ISBN 9780758668530 (paperback) | ISBN 9780758668547 (ebook)

Subjects: LCSH: Witness bearing (Christianity) | Evangelistic work--Lutheran Church. | Lutheran Church--Doctrines.

Classification: LCC BV4520 .W59 2021 (print) | LCC BV4520 (ebook) | DDC 248/.5--dc23

LC record available at https://lccn.loc.gov/2020050532

LC ebook record available at https://lccn.loc.gov/2020050533

1 2 3 4 5 6 7 8 9 10   30 29 28 27 26 25 24 23 22 21

CONTENTS

INTRODUCTION

I'm fascinated by evangelism. I have been for a long time. In some ways, I'm not sure why evangelism captured my attention and has been my passion for many years. But for the most part, I do understand. I understand because I'm a broken person, and I remember when my brokenness took me very far away from the Lord. I remember when my brokenness ruled over me. I remember how my brokenness defined my understanding of myself, of who I was. But more than all that, I remember how God's grace penetrated that brokenness and crushed its lies. I remember how the Good News of Jesus overcame the despair of my brokenness. I remember how the Gospel changed my understanding of myself—how it changed who I am. And I want other broken people to know that joy.

I wish I could say that the Gospel came to me in my brokenness through the faithful witness of someone who had a passion for evangelism. It would be great to tell a story of how someone who knew what it is like to be broken and restored was willing to reach out to me with the Good News that there is a Healer who loves me. The truth is, there were some people who tried to witness to me, but they didn't really know how to share God's Word with broken people. They were sincere, but they were misguided. They weren't telling me that there is Good News for broken people. Instead, they were laying a heavier load on me with the "shoulds" and "musts" of God's Law. I was drowning, and they were handing me bricks.

Thankfully, God's Word always accomplishes what He purposes for it (Isaiah 55:11). That Word had been implanted in my heart in the waters of Holy Baptism. His Word was taught to me as a child when I attended worship and Sunday School. That Word remained with me even though I had given my life over to my brokenness and ventured far away from the Lord, like the prodigal son in Jesus' parable (Luke 15). And His Word brought me back home when it broke through that brokenness with His grace, forgiveness, and healing.

I'm still a broken person. But I'm a broken person living with the hope and joy that comes with the healing that Jesus alone provides. I'm also a broken person who wants other broken people to know His healing. I'm not a super-evangelist. I'm not even a super-Christian. I'm weak; I stumble. I sin in the things I do and in the things I fail to do. I fall short as a husband, father, grandfather, pastor, and friend. I'm broken, and I daily depend on Jesus and His grace to deal with my brokenness.

I suspect that you are a broken person too. In fact, I know you are a broken person. I know this because we are all broken and we all need Jesus to heal us. We are just as broken as the lost people of the world, but we know the Healer. And because we know Jesus' love, joy, and peace, we want other broken people to know the Healer too.

Broken people bringing Good News of the Healer to other broken people. That's how I see evangelism. And that's what makes evangelism my passion. You may see evangelism very differently. Far from your passion, evangelism may seem like a burdensome task to you. It may be more of a source of frustration, fear, and guilt than a source of joy in your life. You may feel inadequate as an evangelist or even convinced that you are not an evangelist. Given all the misguided ideas about evangelism, it's understandable if you feel this way. My hope and prayer in writing this book is to help Christians discover or rediscover the joy of being Christ's witnesses.

Evangelism may not fascinate you, and it may not become your passion (though I hope that it does!), but sharing the Good News of Jesus should be something that you willingly, actively, and effectively do as part of being a disciple of Jesus. There's a world full of broken people—including your neighbors, co-workers, friends, and family members—counting on it.

Pastor Mark A. Wood

Part 1

What? Me, a Witness?

CHAPTER 1

WHAT IS (AND ISN'T) A WITNESS?

You will be My witnesses. Acts 1:8

After Jesus had completed His work to save the world by dying on the cross and rising from the tomb, He gathered His disciples and explained how they would carry on His mission after He ascended into heaven. He said, "But you will receive power when the Holy Spirit has come upon you, and you will be My witnesses in Jerusalem and in all Judea and Samaria, and to the end of the earth" (Acts 1:8).

"You will be My witnesses." That doesn't sound like a question, does it? No, it's definitely a statement. Jesus wasn't asking us if we wanted to be His witnesses or if we would try to be His witnesses. He was plainly saying that we are His witnesses. There's no question here. But this statement does raise some questions: What is a witness? What kind of witness am I? Where should I be a witness? To whom should I witness? And there's the big question: How do

I witness? We'll work through these questions in later chapters, but it's important to set the stage by answering the first one: What is a witness?

A witness is someone who can speak to what he or she knows to be true. Witnesses can be found in various settings. In the world, a person may be called to be a witness in a courtroom because she knows about an event or is an expert in a matter before the court. Within the Church, a parent bringing a child to the font to be baptized is being a witness to the promises of God given in Baptism. Where the Church and the world intersect, a Christian seeks to be a witness by sharing God's Word with people who do not confess Jesus. When we're speaking about evangelism, this is the kind of witness we are talking about.

Here's the thing about being a witness: we are all witnesses of something. When you are telling your friend about the health benefits of using essential oils, you are a witness of essential oils. When you explain the reasons that you support a political candidate, you are a witness of that candidate. When you share your experiences, understanding, or insights, you are being a witness of those things. Perhaps the best way to describe a witness is that a witness is someone who speaks about what he knows to be true.

When my grandson Ashton was fourteen years old, our family celebrated Christmas at our home in Missouri. Family members from various parts of the country gathered in our house and enjoyed one another's company, plenty of food, and, of course, plenty of presents. Even though Ashton wanted a new pair of shoes, there were no new shoes for him. Instead there was a gift card for him to use. My wife and daughter were wise enough to let him pick out his own shoes. The day after Christmas, they went shopping. (Being older and wiser, I opted out of the post-Christmas shopping experience.) When they returned home, Ashton's new shoes caught my attention because they were prominently labeled "Witness."

Why would a line of sport shoes be labeled "Witness"? Being curious about the use of this word, I looked up the brand and found an article about the shoes. It explained that the "Witness" marketing campaign and branding of the shoes was a tribute to the greatness of the basketball player LeBron James. It went on to say that the "Witness" campaign was acknowledging the many people around the world who were witnesses of LeBron's athletic abilities and mastery of the game of basketball. Wow, all that from a pair of shoes. No wonder they cost so much!

The shoes serve as a good reminder that we are all witnesses of something. Some people are witnesses of LeBron James's greatness. Other people are witnesses of horrible crimes. Many people are witnesses of themselves and the ideas they have embraced as personal truths. But you are a witness of something far greater and far better. Jesus said, "You will be *My* witnesses." You are a witness of Jesus.

You are called to share God's Word—to speak about Jesus—with people who do not confess Him.

You didn't ask to be a witness of Jesus. You may even be fighting against the idea that you are a witness of Jesus. But because you have been baptized into Christ, you are His witness. There is no question about this. Remember, Jesus was not making a request in Acts 1:8. He was making a statement of fact. Here's another fact: by making you His witness, Jesus has given you a critical role in His mission.

Sent as He Was Sent

*As the Father has sent Me,
even so I am sending you. John 20:21*

Jesus had been very clear about His mission and how He would carry it out, but His disciples didn't understand Him. Even after He had risen from the dead, after they had seen the empty tomb for themselves, and after Mary had reported what Jesus had said to her when she saw Him in His resurrected body, the first Easter evening found them hiding behind locked doors in fear. Jesus had prepared them to continue His mission, but without a radical change they were not going to be His witnesses.

Imagine what it must have been like to be in that room. The air was thick with fear and doubt. The silence of concern and despair was deafening. Every attempt at having a conversation to make sense of the day's events was met with blank looks and demands to keep quiet so they wouldn't be found out. A nervous disciple or two would check the door every so often to make sure it was securely locked. Brokenness ruled.

Enter Jesus. And with Jesus, a radical change. His first word to His fear-filled disciples was "Peace." Then, after assuring them that it truly was Him, He spoke peace to them again. Joy began to displace their fear. But that fear may have come back with a vengeance when Jesus told them, "As the Father has sent Me, even so I am sending you" (John 20:21).

We tend to gloss over this statement. We treat it like a coach's locker-room pep talk. "Come on, guys, let's get out there." Or as if Jesus were trying to get on our calendar. "I'm sending you. Next week is looking good for Me. When's a good time for you?" But it's far more than that. The disciples would have been right to be troubled by Jesus' statement, not because He was sending them but because He was sending them *as the Father had sent Him*.

Think about what it meant for Jesus to be sent by His Father. It meant taking on human flesh and all of the brokenness that comes with it. It meant that He had to empty Himself of His power, glory, and majesty to become like us. It meant that He had to step down from His rightful place of being honored and praised. It meant that He had to live in the sorrow, suffering, and pain that is woven into our fallen world. It meant the cross.

We are being sent as the Father sent Jesus. This means that we can't be His witnesses by simply sending a check to support evangelism. We need to take some risks, endure some hardships, and engage people in their brokenness. This means that we have to step outside of our comfort zones and speak of Jesus with lost people even if it costs us friendships, career opportunities, or our popularity. It means denying ourselves, taking up our crosses daily, and following Jesus (Luke 9:23).

But being sent as the Father sent Jesus is more than struggle and hardship. It includes great joy. Hebrews 11:2 reminds us to look to "Jesus, the founder and perfecter of our faith, who for the joy that was set before Him endured the cross, despising the shame, and is seated at the right hand of the throne of God."

Yes, Jesus is sending us as the Father had sent Him. We will face significant challenges as we seek to be His witnesses in a world that is captive to and ruled over by a hostile and powerful enemy, an enemy who will fight to keep what he thinks he owns. We may experience hardship or loss. We may be hated and mocked. We may bear heavy crosses to be faithful witnesses. We may. But this is certain: joy is set before us. In time or in eternity (or maybe in both), His witnesses will know that joy.

CHAPTER 2

WHY SHOULD I WITNESS?

We live on earth only so that we should be a help to other people. –Martin Luther

I'm but a stranger here, Heav'n is my home;
Earth is a desert drear, Heav'n is my home.
Danger and sorrow stand Round me on ev'ry hand;
Heav'n is my fatherland, Heav'n is my home.
(LSB 748:1)

When we sing "Earth is a desert drear," we're singing something that is absolutely true. This world is fallen. It is filled with all kinds of hardships and suffering. Danger and sorrow are "Round me on ev'ry hand." This is not our home. Heaven is our home. Heaven is where we belong. It's where our Lord wants us to be.

We know this, yet I've often heard Christians say something like "I'm ready to go home and be with Jesus, but I'd rather not go right now." Maybe you've said or thought the same thing. From our perspective, there are good reasons for wanting to remain in this world. We may want to take care of our family, watch our children grow up, attend their weddings, hold our grandchildren one day, and so forth. These are wonderful blessings that bring us and other people great joy.

But none of these earthly joys can compare with the joys of heaven. Our Lord would rather that we be with Him, where there is no sorrow and there are no tears. The God who loves us and has redeemed us and claimed us as His own, who has washed us in Baptism and adopted us as His children, wants us to be with Him. He wants us to be with Him where there is no suffering, no death, no brokenness, no fallenness. Yet here we are, in this fallen and broken world. Why? Why does the Lord leave us in this place of sin and death? There must be a very good reason for a loving and gracious God to keep us in this "desert drear." And there is.

A pastor I know helps his students understand God's reason for keeping us in this world by pointing out that in heaven we will do many of the things that we also do on earth. However, he explains, there will be two things that we cannot do in heaven that we can do on earth. One is sin. The other is to tell lost people about Jesus. Then he'll ask them, "For which of these two things does God leave us in this fallen, broken world?" (Hint: God doesn't leave us here to sin!)

I would guess that most Christians understand that witnessing is one of the reasons that God leaves us in this world. But I wonder how many would agree that witnessing is not just *a* purpose for us being in the world; witnessing is *the* reason that God has us here.

We "are a chosen race, a royal priesthood, a holy nation, a people for His own possession, that you may proclaim the excellencies of Him who called you out of darkness into His marvelous light" (1 Peter 2:9). In a sermon on this text, Martin Luther explained:

> We live on earth only so that we should be a help to other people. Otherwise, it would be best if God would strangle us and let us die as soon as we were baptized and had begun to believe. For this reason, however, he lets us live that we may bring other people also to faith as he has done for us. . . . Everything then should be directed in such a way that you recognize what God has done for you and that you, thereafter, make it your highest priority to proclaim this publicly and call everyone to the light to which you are called.[1]

Notice the extremes to which Luther goes in the words that he uses to explain 1 Peter 2:9. *"Only"* emphasizes that there is no other purpose for us to be in the world than to "bring other people also to faith." *"Everything"* we have and

---

1   "Sermons on 1 Peter, 1523," cited in *The Church Comes from All Nations*, p. 20.

"*everything*" we do is meant to support this purpose, which we carry out by "*proclaim[ing]*" the Gospel publicly.

I'm not a fan of rolling out Greek words to try to impress or persuade people. We have some very faithful English translations of the Bible that don't need any help from me and my limited abilities with Koine Greek.[2] Still, it is helpful to look at the original languages of the Bible, especially when a verse or passage is very important or a little unusual—and 1 Peter 2:9 is both.

The importance of 1 Peter 2:9 is that it makes very clear who we are in Christ Jesus and what we are here to do. We are the people He chose for Himself. He has made us a holy nation (that is, a people set apart for Him). We are part of His royal family. We are a priesthood of believers. What we are and what we are here to do go together. We are here to "proclaim the excellencies of Him who called us out of darkness into His marvelous light." The Greek word translated as "**proclaim**" is *exangelio*. This is the only place in the New Testament where this word is used. It is different from the words used for "preaching" (e.g., *karuxo*, *lalao*). The sense of the word *exangelio* is "to make something widely known." What 1 Peter 2:9 is telling us is that we are God's people, His priests, here in the world to proclaim Jesus—to make Him and His love widely known.

---

2   Koine Greek is the language in which the New Testament was written.

Think about what Luther is saying in his sermon on this passage. What is left after "**only**"? What is included in "**everything**"? Luther is saying that your only purpose for being in the world is so that other people will hear about Jesus from you. Every single thing that God has entrusted to you is meant to be used for this purpose. Whether you are rich or poor, you live in an urban setting or rural setting, you are part of a large family or a member of a small family, you work in an office or run a family business, you have a college education or work in a trade, all that you do and all that you have is centered on being Jesus' witness. Everything that God has entrusted to you has been specifically given to you so that people who do not know Jesus will hear about Jesus from you.

Is Luther overstating his case? Perhaps, but think of it this way: when Luther claims that we are here to be of help to other people, he is drawing on Jesus' summary of "the Law and the Prophets" (Matthew 22:40). Jesus said, "You shall love the Lord your God with all your heart and with all your soul and with all your mind. This is the great and first commandment. And a second is like it: You shall love your neighbor as yourself" (Matthew 22:37–39). Luther went on to explain that the specific help that we are here to give is to help our neighbor hear about Jesus. By "neighbor" he means anyone who is part of our daily lives. Our neighbors include our friends; the people who live in our community; our co-workers and fellow students; the people we interact with when we are shopping, running errands, and carting children to and from activities; members of the clubs we belong to; people we socialize and recreate with; our children's teachers; the parents of their teammates; the adults who coach and instruct them; the people whom we serve in our occupations; our supervisors or employees; and so forth.

The people in our everyday lives are the people whom we are on this earth to serve by "call[ing] everyone to the light to which [we] are called." Heaven may be our home, but we are in this dreary desert because people all around us are perishing and need our help. They need us to "make it [our] highest priority to proclaim [Jesus] publicly." They are the reason we are in this world. They are our mission field.

Our Part in God's Mission

The Son of Man came to seek and to save the lost. Luke 19:10

Jesus clearly stated His mission in Luke 19:10: "The Son of Man came to seek and to save the lost." In love, Jesus came into our world to seek out and to save people who are lost. But what does it mean for a person to be lost? In everyday language, we call something lost when it is not where it is supposed to be. If you leave your wallet at a restaurant and it disappears, you would say that you've lost your wallet. It's not where it's supposed to be (e.g., in your purse or in your back pocket). It's lost.

In much the same way, we can say that people who are not where they are supposed to be spiritually are lost. People are supposed to be in a harmonious relationship with the Lord. He created us to be in fellowship with Him. When sin entered the world through the disobedience of Adam and Eve, that fellowship was broken, and all of mankind was not where it was supposed to be. We were all lost.

Because God the Father loves the world, He sent His Son, Jesus, to seek and to save the lost. He has reconciled us with the Father—that is, He has restored our good relationship with Him. He has paid for the sins of the whole world so that every human being could be in fellowship with the Father.

Jesus has accomplished everything that is necessary for those who are lost to be saved. He wants everyone "to be saved and to come to the knowledge of the truth" (1 Timothy 2:4). In other words, He wants everyone to be in fellowship with Him. But not everyone is. The majority of people in our world are not where they are supposed to be. They are lost.

There are lost people throughout the world. There are lost people in your workplace and classroom. There are lost people in your neighborhood. There are lost people on your sports teams. There are lost people in your clubs and civic organizations. There are probably even lost people in your family. Sadly, there are many lost people around us, even close to us.

Jesus' work to save the world is complete, but His mission to seek and to save the lost continues to this day. In John 20:21–23, Jesus tells us that He is giving us a vital role in His mission: "Jesus said to them again, 'Peace be with you. As the Father has sent Me, even so I am sending you.' And when He had said this, He breathed on them and said to them, 'Receive the Holy Spirit. If you forgive the sins of any, they are forgiven them; if you withhold forgiveness from any, it is withheld.'"

Jesus is sending us into our world as His witnesses. Witnessing is our part in God's continuing mission. As His witnesses we are called to share God's Word with lost people.

Who Are the "Lost"?

We use different words to refer to lost people. Some words, such as *non-Christian* and *unbeliever*, are troublesome because they imply that we can know with certainty whether or not a person has saving faith in Jesus. In some cases, it is clear by someone's confession that they do not believe in Jesus. In other cases, it is not so clear. Also, *unbeliever* is a bit misleading because many people believe in one false god or another.

I often use the term *nonchurched* to describe lost people. *Nonchurched* describes people who are not connected to a Christian church. It describes a behavior rather than an assessment of a person's spiritual condition—though at best, being nonchurched is a very hazardous spiritual condition.

Approximately two-thirds of Americans identify themselves as Christians. Yet only 15 to 18 percent are active in a Bible-based Christian congregation. This means that many of the people who consider themselves to be Christians are nonchurched.

There are two kinds of nonchurched people. *Dechurched* describes people who were once connected to a Christian church, but for one reason or another, they no longer are. Some dechurched people have simply wandered away. Others have left after a hurtful experience. Still others have embraced a different religion or worldview and have rejected the faith.

The other kind of nonchurched person is *unchurched*. An unchurched person is someone who has never been connected to a Christian church. Such a person may belong to a world religion such as Islam, Buddhism, or Judaism. Or he or she may be active in a non-Christian religion such as the Church of Jesus Christ of Latter Day Saints (Mormons) or Jehovah's Witnesses. Or an unchurched person could be an atheist, an agnostic, or "spiritual but not religious."

Whether they are dechurched or unchurched, non-churched people are living apart from Christ and His Church. They are not where they belong. *They are lost.* Being non-churched is not a good place to be. Being nonchurched means being away from Christ. Nonchurched people are captive to Satan; they're controlled by the world, and they're pointlessly living to satisfy their sinful flesh. They are perishing. They are condemned.

Call the lost whatever you want to call them, but always remember that they are in a horrible spiritual condition. They need Jesus—and they need someone to tell them about Jesus. That would be us. Jesus is sending us into the world to share good news with lost and broken people. That's our part in God's mission.

CHAPTER 3

WHEN, WHERE, AND WITH WHOM AM I A WITNESS?

[God] determined allotted periods and the boundaries of their dwelling place. Acts 17:26

The Lord has placed you in the mission field that He planned for you—and for which He has equipped you. God does not act haphazardly. He is orderly, and He is intimately involved in His creation. Things have not been left to chance. He designed your life according to His plans. He knew beforehand where you would live, what kind of society you would live in, your vocations, and the people He would put into your workplace, school, neighborhood, family, and circle of friends and acquaintances.

St. Paul spoke of this in Acts 17. He explained to the members of the Areopagus that God was in control of His creation. Paul said, "The God who made the world and everything in it, being Lord of heaven and earth, does not live in temples made by man, nor is He served by human hands, as though He needed anything, since He Himself gives to all mankind life and breath and everything. And He made from one man every nation of mankind to live on all the face of the earth, having determined allotted periods and the boundaries of their dwelling place" (Acts 17:24–26).

You live in the place, at the time, and with the people of God's choosing. This isn't fatalism. You are not simply a robot acting out a set of programmed instructions. While the Lord has crafted your circumstances, you must make many choices within the context in which He has placed you. This includes the choice of how you will respond to His call to be His witness in the situations He has created for you—and you for them. But remember this: God already knows what choices you will make—and He loves you no matter what your choices are.

That God knows our choices before we make them is part of His foreknowledge. Foreknowledge is different from predestination. If God had predetermined everything in our lives, then we would be robots acting out a set of programmed instructions. But God didn't predetermine everything in our lives. However, He did know every detail of our lives before we were born. He even knew them before the world existed. That is foreknowledge.

God's complete foreknowledge of all things is mind-boggling. Imagine that your life was written out as an algebra equation. If it were something like "x = 3," you would have the answer to your whole life. Even if it had a second variable, like "x + y = 3," you would be able to figure things out pretty easily. If there were ten variables in the equation of your life, you would have to wait until some of them became known before you could know what the others might be.

But your life isn't one or two or ten variables. It is made up of tens of thousands of variables. There's no way you can know what is going to happen in your life because there are too many variables. Even when you know some of them, there are too many left for you to know the rest. But God knows the value of each variable. More than that, God manages the variables so that the results are for your good. Romans 8:28 puts it this way: "And we know that for those who love God all things work together for good, for those who are called according to His purpose."

Don't stop reading Romans 8 at verse 28. Verses 29–30 make it clear that God is at work through all those variables so that all things do work together for your good. "For those whom He foreknew He also predestined to be conformed to the image of His Son, in order that He might be the firstborn among many brothers. And those whom He predestined He also called, and those whom He called He also justified, and those whom He justified He also glorified."

God foreknows things and God predestines things. Your salvation is something that God has predestined (more on that later). Living out your life as one who has been saved by God's grace falls under God's providential foreknowledge. You have many choices to make that will fill in some of the variables. Whatever decisions you make, the Lord will work through them in one way or another to carry out His mission to seek and to save the lost. Over the course of your life you will be in different places, at different times, with different people. But look at where you are right now and the people who are in your life at this moment in time. This is your mission field. This is where the Lord has placed you to be His witness. This is where you are called to share the Gospel.

CHAPTER 4

WHAT KIND OF WITNESS AM I?

But God chose what is foolish in the world to shame the wise; God chose what is weak in the world to shame the strong. 1 Corinthians 1:27

C. F. W. Walther, the first president of The Lutheran Church—Missouri Synod, was a great advocate for the sharing of God's Word with the world by all believers. He recognized that the power of the Gospel was not in the people sharing it but in the Word itself. Not only are the people who share the Gospel powerless to bring someone to faith, in fact, no layperson, commissioned minister, or pastor is either fit or qualified for this work. Walther pointed this out in one of his lectures to seminary students that is included in the book *Law and Gospel*:

> God plants, manages, extends, and sustains His kingdom not directly, but by means of men who are

altogether unfit for this task. . . . Who can measure the greatness of God's love, revealed in the fact that He desires not only to save this apostate world but also even to employ human beings—that is, sinners—for this task? Who can plumb the depths of the wisdom of God, who knows how to accomplish the work of saving people by—of all things—*using other people who are quite unfit and unqualified for this work*?[3]

We are unfit and unqualified to be Christ's witnesses. This is most certainly true! God should have found a better way to bring salvation to lost people. We avoid witnessing out of fear. We don't want to cause any trouble or create any waves in our relationships by talking about Jesus. We are ambivalent about the horrible spiritual condition of our world. We are apathetic about proclaiming His excellencies to the very people whom He has placed into our lives to hear about His marvelous light from us. We have other priorities, we are busy with other interests, we neglect His Word, and we are filled with fears. "What will people think about me?" "What if they bring up my failures?" "What if they ask questions that I can't answer?"

We can be distracted, unmotivated, disinterested, ineffective, and unwilling witnesses of Jesus even though being His witnesses is our purpose for being in the world. And we can be this way even though many people around us are

3 C. F. W. Walther, *Law and Gospel: How to Read and Apply the Bible*, page 42 (emphasis added).

perishing—including people whom we know as our friends, co-workers, neighbors, and family members. Yes, God should have found a better way to bring salvation to lost people. But He chose not to. He chose you to be His witness.

Do you feel "unfit and unqualified" to be Christ's witness? If so, good! You are right where you need to be. This is how God works. He chose what is foolish to shame the wise. He chose the weak to shame the strong. He chose you, unfit and unqualified, to be His witness.

Consider the prophet Balaam (Numbers 22). You're probably not as qualified to be God's spokesperson as he was. After all, he was an official prophet of God. God even spoke directly to him. But when Balaam was way off base, God sent him a message through the donkey he was riding. You may not be a prophet like Balaam, an evangelist like Billy Graham, or a Bible scholar like your pastor, but if God can speak through a donkey, He can certainly speak through you.

It's good to be unfit and unqualified because we have a God who is more than fit and is vastly qualified. The task before us is too great. But our God is greater. He "knows how to accomplish the work of saving people." He does it through unfit and unqualified—and, even at times, unwilling—people just like you and me.

Jesus has entrusted us with the Good News of salvation for the whole world. He meant for this work to be a blessing to us and to others. Unfortunately, somewhere along the way, it seems that sharing the Good News has become bad news for Christians.

Broken People for Broken People

Men, why are you doing these things?
We also are men, of like nature with you,
and we bring you good news, that you should
turn from these vain things to a living God,
who made the heaven and the earth and the
sea and all that is in them. Acts 14:15

A strange thing happened when Paul and Barnabas were witnessing in the city of Lystra. After Paul healed a man who had been crippled from birth, the people of the city called Paul and Barnabas gods and started to worship them by offering sacrifices. The apostles quickly put a stop to things and explained that they were mortal men like everyone else. The only difference between the two apostles and the people of Lystra was that Paul and Barnabas had faith in the "living God, who made the heaven and the earth and the sea and all that is in them"—the God who had healed the crippled man through Paul and who had healed Paul.

When Paul and Barnabas told the people "we also are men, of like nature with you," they were sharing a truth that we often forget when we set our minds on witnessing.

As Christ's witnesses we are no different than the people to whom we bring the Good News. We are broken people "of like nature" with the broken people we go to. We don't look any different from the people of the world. We have many of the same problems that they have. We suffer many of the same hardships. We deal with the same heartbreaks that they experience. We are just as broken as they are. The difference between us and them is that we know the Healer.

As witnesses we are broken people bringing Good News of the Healer to other broken people. We don't have to have our act together. We don't have to have all of the right answers. We are not fit or qualified to do what we are doing. But like Paul and Barnabas, the Healer has called us to share with others what He has done for us and for them. This calling is not a burden, but it is a joyful task. We get to bring the Good News of the Healer to broken and hurting people!

That's not to say that witnessing is without its challenges and disappointments. Sometimes broken people refuse to see that they are broken and need the Healer. Other times, broken people prefer to live in their brokenness and avoid the Healer. In many cases, brokenness has such a strong hold on people that they have lost any hope that the Healer can help them. Witnesses discover, as Paul and Barnabas did, that being broken is a way of life for many people, and they see everything through the lens of their brokenness. What a vivid reminder of how people without

Christ—people who do not know the Healer—live in their brokenness: without hope, without comfort, without forgiveness, without life.

The brokenness of idolatry had such a grip on the people of Lystra that, even though Paul and Barnabas were able to stop them from offering them sacrifices, they were easily persuaded to stone Paul and leave him for dead. They were willing to worship him as a god, but they would not listen to Paul the broken person tell them the Good News of the Healer.

It is to such hopelessly broken people that Jesus has sent us. In our brokenness. And in love.

Motivated by Love

We love because He first loved us. 1 John 4:19

While it's true that many of the broken people of the world hate us and consider the message of the Bible to be foolishness, most nonchurched people don't do much more than dismiss the Christian faith, reject that the Bible is God's Word, and label Christians with undesirable labels. Some lost people actively persecute the Church and seek to do harm to Christians. Maybe you know this all too well because you've been hurt by people simply because you are a Christian.

Why are nonchurched people opposed to the Church and deaf to the message we try to bring to them? One reason is that more and more, the broken people in our world rejoice in their brokenness. They are not open to hearing anything that is contrary to what they want to hear and do. They dismiss the Bible as out of date or otherwise irrelevant. They will respond to anyone who disagrees with them or their life choices with anger, hatred, and even violence. Why should you take risks to witness to such people? Why should you concern yourself with people who have no desire to hear what you have to say? There's only one reason: love.

Jesus told us, "I say to you who hear, Love your enemies, do good to those who hate you. . . . Love your enemies, and do good, and lend, expecting nothing in return, and your reward will be great, and you will be sons of the Most High, for He is kind to the ungrateful and the evil. Be merciful, even as your Father is merciful" (Luke 6:27, 35–36). Isn't that just like Jesus? He calls us to endure the hatred of lost people and to show them love in return so that we might have the opportunity to speak His love to them. He wants us to understand that He loves them just as much as He loves us—and to act as though we truly believe this.

Some people would say that Jesus' call to love the lost people in our lives is a command to love them. In a sense, it is a command. But if it's simply a command, then it is a matter of the Law, and Jesus is making a burdensome demand of us. To better understand what Jesus is saying to us as His witnesses, it helps to remember that love is not a fruit of the Law (something that we do by our own ability), but it is a fruit of the Spirit (something that God does in us through His Means of Grace). It's the very first fruit that Galatians 5:22–23 lists when it tells us that "the fruit of the Spirit is love, joy, peace, patience, kindness, goodness, faithfulness, gentleness, [and] self-control."

Another thing to keep in mind when wrestling with this call to love lost people is that the lost people we are called to witness to are already people we love (or at least know and care about). They may be enemies of the cross, but we know them as our friends, neighbors, co-workers, fellow students, teammates, and family members. Yes, some of these people have made it clear that they are not open to hearing God's Word from us. You may have had a bad experience from trying to witness to some of them in the past. Your relationship may even have been strained because of it. But no one needs to command you to love them—though you may need an occasional reminder to do so.

Love the nonchurched people in your life, even the ones who are hostile to the Gospel, because Christ loved you. Love them with His love. Love them by showing them the mercy that they do not deserve—just as the Father has shown you mercy that you don't deserve. Don't let the call to love those who don't confess Jesus become a burdensome demand of the Law. Focus on the Gospel.

And never forget that witnessing flows from the love of Christ.

> Now may our Lord Jesus Christ Himself, and God our Father, who loved us and gave us eternal comfort and good hope through grace, comfort your hearts and establish them in every good work and word. 2 Thessalonians 2:16-17

Part 2

How Do I

Witness?

There isn't a "right way" to do evangelism. We need to consider many factors in order to be effective witnesses of Jesus, including the cultural norms of the people we engage, the nature of the relationships that we have with them, our past experiences with them, what (if any) religious beliefs they already have, their openness to talking about spiritual matters, their attitude about sin, and more. What is effective in one setting may be ineffective in another. What may open the door to sharing the Gospel in one context may close it in another.

Witnessing is contextual. The message never changes, but how it is delivered needs to change to address the situation in which we are witnessing. Witnessing is also relational. It involves engaging people with whom we have (or will have) relationships. If you are going to be a faithful and effective witness, you need to address both the contextual and the relational dimensions of evangelism.

How do you do that?

One way to do that is to use a framework for faithful and effective witnessing based on 1 Corinthians 3:5–9. In this passage, after discussing the various divisions in the

Corinthian Church, the apostle Paul puts witnessing into perspective by using an illustration from farming:

> What then is Apollos? What is Paul? Servants through whom you believed, as the Lord assigned to each. I planted, Apollos watered, but God gave the growth. So neither he who plants nor he who waters is anything, but only God who gives the growth. He who plants and he who waters are one, and each will receive his wages according to his labor. For we are God's fellow workers. You are God's field, God's building.

Drawing on the image from farming that Paul used to explain our roles in witnessing, let's explore contextual and relational witnessing as Plowing, Planting, Watering, Waiting Expectantly, and Harvesting.

CHAPTER 5

HOW DO I WITNESS?—PLOWING

Whoever blesses his neighbor with a loud voice, rising early in the morning, will be counted as cursing. Proverbs 27:14

We want people to know about Jesus and to experience His grace. But many people are simply not ready to hear the Good News that we have to share. Sadly, a large number of people in our society are not interested in discussing spiritual matters. Instead, they are focused on the things of this world. They fill up their lives with material goods, sports, recreation, partying, community service, entertainment, and all kinds of other things that they hope will bring them meaning, purpose, and joy. It's not that these things are bad in and of themselves. Using them properly, we can enjoy them all as good gifts from the Lord. But their improper use often leads to them becoming idols—they end up taking the place of God in people's lives.

When an idol has taken hold of a person's life, we have work to do before we can have an effective witnessing conversation with that person. In farming terms, such a person is hard soil that needs cultivating; that is, it needs plowing. If we don't spend some time and effort plowing, we are likely to experience what Proverbs 27:14 describes. What we share as a blessing will be heard as a curse—or as a meaningless nuisance.

When I was in the Air Force, I played on the base soccer team. One of the other players, Vince, was a recent convert to the Christian faith. He was very excited about sharing the Gospel, but he was also very misguided in his witnessing approach. I remember one time when he left our practice session to stand on the sidewalk and shout "Jesus loves you!" at the passing cars. His message was true. But his delivery made it into something strange and unwanted. The blessing was heard as a curse.

We have our own ways of making the blessing into a curse in the ears of the people we are witnessing to. We may say something that is insensitive, reopen an old wound, come across as overbearing, be heard as judgmental, or blurt out something that was better left unsaid. These and other witnessing mistakes can be avoided if we help people get ready to hear God's Word by plowing the hardened soil of their hearts.

How do we plow the hard soil of lost people's hearts?

Let's look at five things we can do to cultivate our relationships in order to be more aware of witnessing opportunities and to be better prepared to speak God's Word in a way that other people are more open to hearing and discussing:

- Recognize the lost people God has put into your life.
- Pray for the lost people in your life . . . and for yourself as a witness.
- Understand how the other person connects and communicates.
- Listen to learn and understand the other person's story.
- Ask questions that encourage the other person to share more.

Recognize the Lost People God Has Put into Your Life

I often run into Christians who tell me that they don't know any lost people. When I hear that, I start asking about the people in their lives to help them see that there are non-churched people in different parts of their everyday lives. These different parts of our lives are called our "vocations."

A vocation is a calling. Every Christian has callings from the Lord. These callings can be—and often are—very different, but they fall into four categories. We call these four categories the "realms," or areas, of our vocations. They are:

- Family
- Occupation
- Neighbor
- Church

The four realms of our vocations are not four separate divisions of our lives. They are four different contexts in which we live out our lives that typically overlap to one degree or another. The time, energy, and money we expend is not equally divided among the four areas of our vocations. How we spend them varies throughout our lives. These four realms of vocation are the order and structure of our lives—the ways in which God has arranged our lives to be of service to Him and other people.

The Family realm speaks to your role as a child, spouse, parent, sibling, cousin, aunt or uncle, grandparent, in-law, and so forth in your relationships with family members during your life. Within a family you are connected to many other people. It's unlikely that all of those people are Christians. The sad reality of our world is that we don't have to go very far in our family tree before we encounter nonchurched people. Who are the lost people in your family?

The realm of Occupation encompasses our roles as workers, employers, business owners, students, stay-at-home parents, retirees, and so forth. For much of our lives, the realm of Occupation consumes a great deal of our time and energy. But it also puts us into contact with many people who don't know Jesus. In our workplaces, marketplaces, and schools, we are in the midst of many, many nonchurched people. They are our co-workers, fellow students, customers, vendors, teachers, fellow retirees. It's true that the realm of Occupation comes with some witnessing challenges and restrictions, but it's also true that we are called by the Lord into our occupations to be His witnesses. Who are the non-churched people in your occupation?

The realm of Neighbor is a very extensive area of our lives. It involves what we do as citizens, members of a community, and residents in a neighborhood. Your vocation as a Neighbor includes your involvement in public activities ranging from what you do as a volunteer in a civic organization or your children's school to getting together with the people who live on your block for a cookout. The people in this area of your vocation include people who live near you, the people you recreate with, your children's coaches and teammates, other members of clubs or groups you belong to, the families of your children's friends, civil servants, and people in your community who are in need of food, clothing, and shelter. Who are your nonchurched neighbors?

The realm of Church may seem like a very unlikely place to encounter lost people. It is if we limit our understanding of church to the times we gather with other believers for worship or Bible study. When we start to consider the people whom we engage in the roles that we have as members of a congregation, we see that through this realm of vocation, we encounter nonchurched people through our mercy work, human care, social ministry, and congregational outreach activities. Think about the things that you do as a member of your congregation and the people you serve through those activities. Consider the spouses and family members of the people you worship with who aren't in church with them. Picture the people who used to be active in worship and Bible study who have been absent for a while. Who among them is nonchurched?

Pray for the Lost People in Your Life . . . and for Yourself as a Witness

Jesus tells us that prayer is an important part of witnessing. As He sent His disciples out to the villages He was about to visit, Jesus told them, "The harvest is plentiful, but the laborers are few. Therefore pray earnestly to the Lord of the harvest to send out laborers into His harvest" (Luke 10:2).

We should pray for those who labor to bring the Good News to people (that would be us), and we should pray for the people who will hear God's Word from us or other witnesses.

As important as prayer is for witnessing, prayer is not witnessing. We cannot pray people into faith. Prayer does not change people's hearts; only God's Word can do that. As Romans 10:17 tells us, "Faith comes from hearing, and hearing through the word of Christ." The Augsburg Confession echoes this in Article V: the Holy Spirit "works faith, when and where it pleases God [John 3:8], in those who hear the good news" (AC V:3). Prayer does not save lost people.

So why should we pray? Prayer prepares us as witnesses. When we pray, we are acknowledging that we are not able to do what we desire to do. We cannot save people. We are totally dependent on the Lord to bring lost people to faith. We pray for the right words to say, for the understanding to know the best way to approach a person, for wisdom to see opportunities for witnessing, for protection from the enemy who fights against Christ's witnesses, for the discernment we need to properly share Law and Gospel, and for the aid of the Holy Spirit. We have a lot to pray for as witnesses.

We also want to pray for the people to whom we are witnessing or want to witness. We can pray that the Word that we share with them will take root and grow. We can include them and their concerns in our prayers of intercession. We can also pray that they will be open to having a conversation about Jesus with us. And we should certainly pray that the Lord of the harvest would send His laborers to them to fearlessly, boldly, and lovingly speak His Word of life to them. As we pray for the lost people in our lives, we should be keenly aware that our prayers are heard by and are pleasing to our Father in heaven, who wants all people to be saved. But we should be just as keenly aware that our prayers will not save them. They need to hear the Word.

Understand How the Other Person Connects and Communicates

People connect and communicate in different ways. Some people prefer to discuss things on an intellectual level and love the give-and-take of a good discussion (maybe even a good argument). Other people don't enjoy debating ideas but are more in tune with how people feel about things. And others are less interested in talking about things than they are in doing things. Knowing how a person prefers to connect and communicate is very helpful when engaging a person in a witnessing conversation. I like to talk about these three ways of connecting and communicating as "Head," "Heart," and "Hands."

"Head" people tend to focus on truth. They like to discuss ideas, and they enjoy evaluating, analyzing, and debating concepts. They are not very concerned about how people feel about things. They are more interested in the value of an idea as an idea worth consideration and contemplation. A "Head" person is likely to say "I think . . ." when you are speaking with him or her.

"Heart" people are centered on the emotional understanding of things. This doesn't mean that they don't think about ideas; it means that they think about them in a very different way than "Head" people do. They focus on how an idea impacts a person's emotional well-being and shapes a person's sense of value, belonging, and acceptance. You'll hear a "Heart" person repeatedly say, "I feel . . . ."

"Hands" people look at things from a practical perspective. They don't want to talk—they want to act. They want to know how to put an idea into actions that will make a positive difference in people's lives, in their communities, or in the world. "Hands" people love projects. They tend to embrace or dismiss an idea based on its practical implications. People who say "I do . . ." or "I should . . ." are likely to be "Hands" people.

Keep in mind that we are all "Head," "Heart," *and* "Hands" people. However, everyone has a preference toward one of these ways of connecting and communicating. Understanding how the other person prefers to connect and communicate will help you be an effective witness. Once you understand the other person's preference, you should work at connecting and communicating with him or her in that way.

This means that you may have to set aside your preference and take up the preference of the other person.

How can you tell if someone is a "Head," "Heart," or "Hands" person? The best way is to listen to the other person. Listening is an important first step in being a witness of Jesus. This may be surprising to you because many witnessing approaches of the past focused on speaking rather than listening. Witnessing in today's context needs to start with listening because we can't assume anything about the other person's knowledge of or interest in spiritual matters. With so many different worldviews and religious ideas in our culture, we have no way of knowing what a person knows or believes until we listen to him. By truly listening to a person, you not only figure out whether he is a "Head," "Heart," or "Hands" person, but you also learn and understand his story.

Listen to Learn and Understand the Other Person's Story

In James 1:19 we are told to be "quick to hear." Listening is a great way to start a witnessing conversation for a number of reasons. In the first place, listening enables us to obtain information about a person from a very authoritative source— the person! If you want to get to know a person, listen to the person. There's an adage that goes, "You're not learning anything when you're talking." It's amazing what we learn when we listen.

Listening to people can be very enjoyable. Whether it's learning an interesting fact from someone's experience or discovering something that you have in common with a person, through listening we can gain a real and lasting connection with someone that brings us genuine joy. Part of that joy comes when listening to another person opens us up to discovering more about him as a person. We may have had a relationship with someone for a long time, but we have never really gotten to know her because we have never really listened to her. Interesting and informative perspectives, experiences, life lessons, and more are often waiting to be discovered by listening.

As Christ's witnesses, listening is our primary tool for understanding what a person thinks about religion, feels about spiritual matters, wants to accomplish with her life, considers to be important (and not important), and so forth. Without first listening to the other person, we are left with our own assumptions about that person—assumptions that are often inaccurate and almost always hinder our witness rather than help it.

It's one thing to recognize the need to be a good listener and another thing to actually listen well. For most of us, being a good listener is challenging. One reason it's difficult for us to effectively listen to other people is that we've never been taught to listen well. Good listening skills do not come naturally to most people. It takes work and intentional effort to listen well.

There are many resources to help us become better listeners. You should have no trouble finding books, podcasts, seminars, and courses on effective listening. Here are a few of the suggestions that these resources typically promote.

Listen to listen, not to form a response. It's hard to listen to another person and not start thinking about what you want to say in response to what he is saying. But as soon as you start forming a response, you've stopped listening. Focus on what is being said, and push aside the tendency to craft a brilliant reply. If you keep listening, you may very well discover that the reply you might have made wasn't all that brilliant after all.

Remove distractions. We may live in an age in which multitasking is considered normal, but it is becoming more apparent that we aren't very good multitaskers. In order to effectively listen to someone, we need to focus on what she is saying by making listening the one and only thing that we are doing. This means putting away our devices, turning off the television, stepping away from the computer, finding a child-free time to have a conversation, or removing whatever else may be a distraction to you.

As people speak, listen with your whole body. Only part of what people say is communicated in audible words. Much of what is being said is spoken through body language. Facial expressions, posture, voice inflection, and eye contact are part of the conversation—not only for the person speaking but also for the person listening. Make sure that your body language shows that you are listening.

Don't interrupt the person speaking. Interrupting a person while he is speaking is essentially shouting, "I'm not really listening to you!" Fight the temptation to finish a sentence, help with a word choice, correct grammar or pronunciation, or object to something that has been said. Instead, keep listening.

Provide feedback. This may sound like a contradiction to the "don't interrupt" advice above, but remember that much of how we communicate doesn't involve words. Use body language such as nodding, eye contact, smiling or frowning, raising your eyebrows, and adjusting your posture to show that you are listening and engaged. You may even use a short verbal cue such as "uh-huh" or "okay" to reinforce that you are listening.

Listen through the silence. One of the most difficult things to do when listening to a person is to keep quiet during silence. People use silence to collect their thoughts, to search for the right words to express something, and to decide what to share or not to share. Listening through the silence gives the other person the opportunity to keep speaking—and for you to keep listening.

One more thing about listening. People in our culture are starving for people to listen to them. In our setting of being constantly bombarded with messages, it's rare to find someone who is willing and able to listen well. If you work at being a good listener, you will have no shortage of people willing to share their stories with you. And you will be conveying a very important and very welcome message by listening: "I care about you as a fellow human being."

Ask Questions That Encourage the Other Person to Share More

Ask" pairs nicely with "Listen" because asking questions encourages people to continue speaking, which provides further opportunities to listen. Asking good questions is a powerful way to learn more about a person's worldview, spiritual perspectives, knowledge of God's Word, concerns about life, and a host of other topics. When it comes to learning more about a person, questions are always more effective than statements. Asking good questions also shows people that we are interested in them as people, not as objects of conquest.

Questions encourage discussion more than statements do. Answering a question stimulates people to think about a topic more deeply than responding to a statement does. Statements tend to focus a conversation on a point or topic, but questions open up a universe of possibilities. In addition to learning a person's needs, concerns, and desires, asking questions can also help clear up any misunderstandings that come up because of terminology or ideas that may be confusing to you.

Each witnessing situation is different. The questions you ask a person and the flow of the questions will vary. This means that having a script of questions prepared before the conversation is not very effective. Asking "canned" questions will probably come off as artificial and impersonal. It's good to have a few go-to questions that you can ask in different situations, but whenever possible, ask questions that come to you as you listen to the other person's story. Keep in mind that the goal of asking good questions is to keep your conversation going so you can actively listen to the other person to discern how best to serve her as a witness of Jesus.

Good questions will encourage the other person to keep speaking. Good questions will also show the person that you are listening to him and are genuinely interested in what he is sharing. What makes for a good question? Let's look at the characteristics of good questions and some examples that might come from a conversation in which you are speaking with someone who doesn't believe in God but is angry with Him for permitting evil in the world.

Good questions flow from the conversation. Questions that come to your mind as you listen to or reflect on what the other person has shared with you encourage him to share more. A question that comes out of left field and is not clearly related to the conversation you're having is likely to be received with suspicion. This is one reason that scripted or "canned" questions aren't very effective. Listen well, and good questions will come to you. When they do, fight the temptation to interrupt the other person. Hold on to the questions and ask them when he has finished speaking. A good question to ask in our example conversation might be the following:

> *What kinds of evil things in our world are especially troubling to you?*

Good questions are open-ended. An open-ended question is one that can't be answered with a short answer such as yes or no; that would be a closed-ended question. Closed-ended questions don't encourage people to speak beyond that short reply. Closed-ended questions are often used to make statements into questions rather than to ask a genuine question. Closed-ended questions can be conversation killers. Open-ended questions, on the other hand, encourage conversation. They call for an extensive answer. Open-ended questions also convey a sincere interest in what the other person has to say. Consider the two following questions that could be asked in the same conversation, and you'll see how the open-ended question is much better for continuing a conversation:

> *Closed-ended question: Based on what you've told me so far, I can see that you are angry with God about allowing evil in the world, right?*

> *Open-ended question: I'm hearing that you're angry with God because He allows evil in the world. How do you think God is dealing with your anger with Him?*

Good questions are personal but not invasive. A good question is tailored to the person you are listening to; it is about her or something she has shared. However, the question shouldn't be invasive by being too personal. The boundaries of what makes a personal but not invasive question are set by your relationship with the other person. You can ask a close friend a more personal question than you can ask a new acquaintance. In our sample conversation, you could ask one of these questions, based on the closeness of your relationship:

> *With a close friend: What evil things has God allowed to happen to you?*

> *With a new acquaintance: What evil things have you seen happen to people that you think God shouldn't have allowed?*

Good questions don't require the other person to give a "right" or "wrong" answer. The questions we're asking as witnesses are meant to keep a conversation going.

Asking questions that imply there's a "right" or "wrong" answer will likely come across as a test (or even as an inquisition) and will tend to close down the conversation. Be careful of falling into the trap of using questions to make statements. Witnessing questions are not meant to share or teach the faith. They are meant to help us learn about and understand the other person so we can share and teach the faith effectively when that opportunity arises. In the meantime, especially while listening and asking to learn someone's story, it's okay for him to be "wrong" in his answer—in fact, it is helpful to you as a witness to hear a person's "wrong" answers. Be careful to avoid a question that makes a person feel like he is trapped in a corner by having to respond with a "right" answer.

> *Implies a "right" or "wrong" answer: Since God is all powerful, can't He make good things happen through the evil He allows?*

> *Encourages discussion: How might something good come out of the evil that God allows to happen in a person's life?*

Good questions take into consideration whether the other person is a "Head," "Heart," or "Hands" person. Asking a question that takes into account how the other person prefers to connect and communicate not only encourages the person to respond, it also shows that you've been listening. Listening will help you figure out whether a person is a "Head," "Hands," or "Heart" person. Once you've figured that out, it isn't difficult to frame your questions accordingly. In the same way that a "Head" person will say, "I think . . . ," she is likely to respond more readily to a question that asks, "What do you think about . . . ?" Likewise, a "Heart" person is more open to questions that ask about his feelings, and a "Hands" person, about what he would do. In a conversation with someone who is angry with God over evil in the world, you could ask a question tailored for "Head," "Heart," or "Hands" as follows:

> *"Head" person: Why do you think God allows evil in the world?*

> *"Heart" person: How does it make you feel when God allows evil in the world?*

> *"Hands" person: What would you like to do about the evil that God allows in our world?*

Good questions are questions that you may not know the answers for. A great way to learn more about another person is to ask her a question that has an answer that you don't know. Not only does a question such as this encourage the other person to share parts of her story that you don't know, but it also shows sincere interest in her and her story. The context of your conversation and the nature of your relationship are important guides to what kinds of questions you can ask (remember to be personal but not invasive). It is especially effective to use open-ended questions such as the following one when asking about something you don't know:

How has the evil in our world been particularly troubling to you?

Good questions encourage the other person to speak more. The point of asking questions is to listen to the other person. Practically speaking, a question that helps him share more of his story is a good question to ask. There is no end to the questions that you can ask a person, but there is likely to be a limit to how many questions a person is willing to answer. By listening attentively, you'll know if the person is reaching that limit. You'll also know when the opportunity to stop cultivating and start planting has come.

CHAPTER 6

HOW DO I WITNESS?—PLANTING

And when His disciples asked Him what this parable meant, [Jesus] said, "To you it has been given to know the secrets of the kingdom of God, but for others they are in parables, so that 'seeing they may not see, and hearing they may not understand.' Now the parable is this: The seed is the word of God." Luke 8:9-11

Planting through a Point of Connection

There is so much to say about Jesus that it can be hard to find a place to start. But because there is so much to say about Jesus, there's something in Jesus' story to share with everyone. You can be confident that there is something in Jesus' story that relates to the person you are conversing with because Jesus' story connects to every human being.

Your challenge as His witness is to determine something to share that is meaningful for and interesting to the other person. You can do that by seeking out a point of connection between Jesus' story and the other person's story.

It's very important to recognize that the point of connection you are looking for is not how *you* are connected to the person, but it is something in her life that connects her story and Jesus' story. That connection may not be something that you have in common with the other person. That's okay. It still provides a way for you to continue the conversation and to make that conversation about Jesus.

We discover points of connection with Jesus' story when people relate positive or negative life events, express concerns, share a need, state a doubt, explain a worldview, or tell us about experiencing a loss. It is likely that the person you are engaging has multiple points of connection with Jesus' story.

Finding a point of connection comes from listening to the other person share his story. As you listen to him and ask good questions, you will learn more about him and his interests, likes, dislikes, fears, concerns, and hopes. It's in these things that you will discover a starting point for speaking about Jesus in a way that connects with him.

When You Plant, Plant the Word

In the parable that Jesus told in Matthew 13, He painted a word picture of how we should go about being His witnesses. He described a farmer going out to sow seed in his field. In that field there were four kinds of soil. Some was hard packed, some was shallow, some was filled with weeds, and some was good soil; that is, it was well cultivated. As the farmer cast the seed by hand, seeds fell onto each kind of soil. Keep in mind that the farmer was sowing the seed generously, not recklessly. To be generous with the seed, he didn't slow down to carefully select the soil before sowing.

As the parable continues, we learn that only the seed that ended up in the good soil produced anything. When Jesus explained the parable to His disciples, He made it clear that there was nothing wrong with the seed. The same good seed was sown onto all four kinds of soil. He also explained that the seed represents the Word of God, and the soil, the different kinds of people who hear the Word of God.

In this rich word picture there is much to overlook. One thing that people often miss is that the parable begins with the farmer sowing and assumes that the farmer had already prepared the field for sowing. The first hearers of this parable would have understood right away that the soil had been cultivated beforehand. And they would have understood that even after cultivating the field, there would still be these four kinds of soil. As Christ's witnesses we should be aware that all four kinds of soil will still be present in the lives of the people we witness to, even after our best "plowing" efforts. While we can approach witnessing in a way that will make people more open to listening to us, we cannot make people more receptive to the Word of God.

Another thing that people can miss is that the focus of the parable is on the seed, not on the soil. This is an important point because it keeps our focus on sharing God's Word rather than on testing the soil. It encourages us to be generous in our planting because we know that God's Word is good and that God's Word is abundant. Following the farmer's example, we can share God's Word generously with the confidence that the Lord will bring forth a harvest. What a beautiful way of restating God's promise in Isaiah 55:10–11, "For as the rain and the snow come down from heaven and do not return there but water the earth, making it bring forth and sprout, giving seed to the sower and bread to the eater, so shall My word be that goes out from My mouth; it shall not return to Me empty, but it shall accomplish that which I purpose, and shall succeed in the thing for which I sent it."

As a witness of Jesus, you are a sower of His Word. Do your plowing to cultivate the soil, but don't hesitate to sow generously. And when you plant, plant God's Word.

Planting God's Word Is Sharing Jesus' Story

There are many things that we can share with lost people, but there is only one thing we can share that will change a person from spiritually dead to spiritually alive. Not even the most convincing human argument nor the strongest worldly consolation nor the grandest undertaking of mankind can do this. Only the Word of Christ can bring life to those who are dead in their trespasses and sins. It is the only thing we have to share that can and does change people's hearts. Sharing His Word with people is our goal and our desire as His witnesses.

Sharing God's Word with people involves more than spouting off a bunch of Bible passages like some kind of "robo-witness" or handing a person some printed material and hoping that he'll read it. Sharing God's Word effectively involves listening, asking, and looking for a point of connection in order to understand which passages of the Bible are most applicable to the person and how best to share them with her. It always means speaking the truth in love—including sharing God's Law in love! It often means that we need to craft a story that the person can understand and relate to. When we do, we need to be careful to avoid making witnessing about sharing "my story."

A persistent bad idea about witnessing is that witnessing is telling other people "what God has done for me"—in other words, to tell people "my story." I consider this a bad idea because it makes witnessing about me. Your story may be very interesting and compelling, especially if you lived an open and active sinful life before coming to faith in Jesus. On the other hand, your story may be rather ordinary. Like many Christians, you may have been born into a family with faithful parents who brought you to the waters of Holy Baptism when you were an infant, and there's never been a time in your life when you didn't know Jesus. Either way, your story isn't going to save anyone. There's only one saving story: Jesus' story.

When we share a story as witnesses, we need to share Jesus' story. Sometimes telling "my story" is a great way to get to Jesus' story. Sometimes it just gets in the way of His story. Sharing "my story" is optional. Sharing Jesus' story is essential. As a faithful witness, strive to keep things about Jesus by sharing His story.

Planting Is Speaking the Truth in Love

In Ephesians 4:15 we are told to speak the truth in love. What does it mean to speak the truth in love? In the first place, it means that we speak the truth. It is not loving to tell people things that are not true or to withhold the truth from them because we are concerned that the truth will make them uncomfortable (or make us uncomfortable). It also means that when we do speak the truth of God's Word, we do so in a way that is respectful and caring. We don't use the truth as a club to overpower people. And we don't speak down to people when sharing God's Word or make them feel inadequate because they don't know what we know about the Bible.

Speaking the truth in love also means telling people what they need to hear even when it is not what they want to hear. Of course, everyone needs to hear the Gospel in order to be saved, and we are eager to speak God's Word of grace to people. But some people need to hear the Law in order to understand their need for the Gospel. This brings up an important question for us as Christ's witnesses: Which is truth, Law or Gospel? The answer to that question is easy. Both Law and Gospel are truth because both Law and Gospel are God's Word. The more challenging question for you as Jesus' witness is, When do you share the Law and when do you share the Gospel?

Knowing when to share the Law and when to share the Gospel isn't cut and dried because it depends on what the other person needs to hear. For this, consider what you have heard from him when you were listening to his story and asking questions to learn more. Through listening and asking, you will learn how he understands his sinful condition and his broken relationship with God. If he is comfortable with his sins or thinks that he is a good-enough person just as he is, you should start sharing Jesus' story from the Law. However, if he is troubled by his sins or understands that there is nothing good in him, you should start sharing Jesus' story from the Gospel. Learning the other person's story will guide you in determining whether you should start with sharing the Gospel or start with sharing the Law. Either way, speak the truth in love.

Speaking the Law in Love

It's not surprising that most of us don't find speaking the Gospel in love to be very difficult. After all, the Gospel is the Good News of God's love given to us in Jesus Christ. But speaking the Law in love sounds daunting. However, there are times when speaking the Law "with gentleness and respect" is the most loving thing that we can do. Consider Jesus' encounter with the wealthy young man who was caught up in works-righteousness:

> [Jesus said,] "You know the commandments: 'Do not murder, Do not commit adultery, Do not steal, Do not bear false witness, Do not defraud, Honor your father and mother.'" And he said to Him, "Teacher, all these I have kept from my youth." And Jesus, looking at him, loved him, and said to him, "You lack one thing: go, sell all that you have and give to the poor, and you will have treasure in heaven; and come, follow Me." (Mark 10:19–21)

Note carefully verse 21 in this passage. Jesus looked at the young man, loved him, and then spoke the Law very clearly and pointedly. Jesus spoke the Law in love. He knew by listening to the man that he was comfortable with his sins and felt that he was good enough for God. Jesus could have argued with him ("How could you have kept all these commandments perfectly from your youth?") or pummeled him with God's Law to show him what a terrible sinner he was ("What? Are you saying you never even looked at or thought about a woman with desire? You've never been angry with your brother? never argued with your father or mother?"). But He saw a way to speak the Law that did not crush the man. He spoke the Law in love so that the man would hear it and take it in, even if doing so did not immediately open the way for the Gospel.

Don't overlook the importance of Jesus not sharing the Gospel in this encounter. Based on the man's response, Jesus ended the conversation with the Law. I have no doubt that Jesus wanted the man to hear the Gospel. And that's why He didn't share the Gospel. He knew that the man could not hear the Gospel until the Law had done its work. There will be times when you as Christ's witness will not find a way to share the Gospel with someone. When that happens, remember this encounter between Jesus and the rich young man. If Jesus, who is the ultimate witness, was willing to end a conversation with the Law, you should be willing to do so too.

The Selfie Mirror of the Law

You may be thinking, "Well sure, *Jesus* knew how to speak the Law in love. He's the Son of God. He can do anything." In a way, you have an advantage over Jesus when it comes to speaking the Law in love. Jesus spoke the Law as the Holy One of God, but you speak the Law as one who has broken it and knows the guilt of being a sinner. When you share the Law with a person, you are speaking as someone who is just as broken and sinful as the person you are speaking with. Apart from the grace of God, you are no different than she is. You can share the Law in love because you are a broken person bringing the Good News of the Healer to another broken person.

Like many pastors, when I teach people Law and Gospel from the Small Catechism, I explain the three different "uses" of the Law by illustrating them as a curb, a mirror, and a guide. Witnessing primarily involves the second "use" of the Law, as a mirror that shows us our sins. This word picture of the Law is helpful for understanding how to share the Law in love by comparing two ways to use the mirror of the Law.

The first way that we can use the mirror of the Law is to hold it up in front of people in a manner that says, in so many words, "Look at you! The Word of God tells you that you are a sinner. See, the mirror of the Law shows you just as you are.

It reveals your sins." These statements are absolutely true. But are they loving?

The second way that we can use the mirror of the Law is to hold it up as we would a cell phone camera for a selfie. Holding up the Law in this way says, "Look at us! The Word of God shows us that we are sinners. It reveals us just as we are. It reveals our sins." Not only are these statements true, but they are loving.

How are these two approaches different? The first comes across as harsh and judgmental because it makes the person feel singled out, as if he is sinful and you are not. By including yourself, the second approach conveys that you are just as sinful and broken as the other person without coming across as judgmental.

As a witness of Jesus, there may be times when you will need to hold up the mirror of the Law and let it crush a person who is so entrenched and comfortable in his sins that he needs to feel the full force of God's Law. But in most witnessing situations, holding up the Law as a selfie mirror will do a much better job of showing someone her sins in a way that expresses love—and will keep the conversation about Jesus going.

Let the Law Do Its Work

This brings us to something that is difficult for many of us to do. It's difficult because we are eager to tell people the Good News about Jesus. We want them to know the love and forgiveness that Jesus has for them. But if we rush into the Gospel before letting the Law do its work, we may end up losing the opportunity to speak the Gospel in a way that the other person can hear it. That can happen when the Gospel is spoken before a person understands or feels his need for the Gospel.

When the Law does its work, a person will be convicted of his sins. The Law will accuse and condemn him. He will see that he has no way of escaping the condemnation of the Law through his own efforts. He will recognize that he needs someone to rescue him, or he will have to face God's judgment and wrath. When the Law has done its work, a person will see his sin and see his need for a Savior.

Telling someone the Gospel before the Law has done its work is like offering healthful food to someone who has just eaten a box of cookies. She needs the healthful food, but she doesn't sense her need for it because her hunger has been satisfied by the unhealthy (though yummy!) cookies. Giving the Law time and space to do its work is letting the person develop a hunger for the good food of the Gospel.

I know that some people teach an approach to evangelism that focuses on telling the Gospel to as many people as possible. They don't concern themselves with the Law. Instead, they tell everyone they encounter, "Jesus loves you and died for your sins." They may even support this approach to witnessing by pointing to the parable of the sower and highlighting how the seed was cast onto all kinds of soil. But it's another saying of Jesus that best describes this evangelism approach: "Do not give dogs what is holy, and do not throw your pearls before pigs, lest they trample them underfoot and turn to attack you" (Matthew 7:6).

Telling people who have dismissed the Law or who have no sense that they need forgiveness that Jesus loves them and forgives them is "casting pearls before pigs." It is taking the treasure of the Gospel and giving it to people who will trample it underfoot. And this is what happens when well-intentioned people indiscriminately broadcast the Gospel. Interestingly, they get enough positive response to this approach to make it seem effective. Why do some people respond positively to this approach? Because in one way or another (usually through the earlier witnessing efforts of other Christians), the Law has already done its work in them.

There may be times when you are witnessing to someone you will probably never see again (for instance, when you're talking to someone on an airplane). In such cases, you may want to say something about the Gospel while you have the chance. As someone once put it, you can't force someone to hear your message, but don't underestimate the power of a seed planted. In day-to-day witnessing, you are typically speaking with a person whom you will speak with again. In those ordinary witnessing conversations, don't share the Gospel with someone who doesn't sense his need for it. Have patience, trust that the Holy Spirit is active in the Word that you have shared, and let the Law do its work.

Don't Speak the Law to People Crushed by the Law

There's a time for speaking the Law in love and a time for speaking the Gospel in love. It's critically important to know which time is which. Fortunately, it isn't difficult to discern whether you should be sharing the Law or the Gospel if you've been listening well and asking good questions. When a person tells you that she has been beaten down by the Law, sees how she has fallen short of the glory of God, feels terrible guilt over her failure to follow God's Word, and recognizes that she cannot do anything to make things right with God, the Law has done its work. Don't pile on more Law. In the words of Matthew 12:20, she is a "bruised reed" and a "smoldering wick."

Jesus was described as having care and compassion for the people who, as "bruised reeds" and "smoldering wicks," were already weighed down by sin and guilt. In contrast to the scribes and Pharisees, who crushed such people with more demands, Jesus comforted them and assured them that He had come into the world "not . . . to judge the world but to save the world" (John 12:47). Once the Law has done its work, we would be cruel and uncaring to speak more Law to people. They are ready for and desperately need the Gospel.

Don't Just Speak about the Gospel; Speak the Gospel

When you can see that the Law has done its work in a person's life and he needs to hear the Gospel, make sure that you *speak the Gospel to him*, not just *speak about the Gospel with him*. That sounds like a subtle difference, but it is significant.

Speaking about the Gospel is telling a person something that is wonderful and true but not making it clear that it is for her. For example, telling someone that Jesus died on the cross to take away sins is true, but it may leave her wondering if His death on the cross took away *her* sins. That would be speaking *about* the Gospel *with* her. Speaking the Gospel *to* her would be saying something like "Jesus died on the cross to take away *your* sins. By His blood, all of your sins have been paid for." Sharing the Gospel in this way makes it very clear that it is for her.

A popular idea about witnessing that encourages people to speak about the Gospel rather than speaking the Gospel is that evangelism is telling people what God has done for you. The argument for this approach to witnessing is that it gives us a way to talk about Jesus that is comfortable for us and nonthreatening to other people. I've also heard people explain that this way of witnessing presents a story to people that they cannot say is not true. Unfortunately, in our world, this approach enables people to quickly and easily dismiss how that story, however true, might apply to them. Many people in our culture will see such a story as "your truth," not their truth. They may even say something like "I'm glad that works for you." When you hear that kind of response, you should recognize that you've spoken *about* the Gospel and haven't actually spoken the Gospel *to* the person.

It isn't difficult to shift from speaking about the Gospel to speaking the Gospel. For the most part it involves telling people the Gospel we know so well in a way that says, "This Gospel is for you too." It's telling people Jesus' story so that they can see how His story includes their story. It may or may not include telling people "what God has done for me," but it always includes a clear message of what God has done for the other person. When we are able to share the Gospel in this way, we have done all that we can do to plant the seed of the Word. But it isn't the end of our efforts to witness to a person. Once we've planted the seed, we need to water it. That is, we need to tend to the soil and nurture what has been planted there.

CHAPTER 7

HOW DO I WITNESS?—WATERING

*Whoever brings blessing will be
enriched, and one who waters will
himself be watered. Proverbs 11:25*

We can plant the seed of God's Word, but we cannot make it grow. But that doesn't mean that we should forget about the seed once we've sown it. Like a farmer doing what he can do to produce a good crop, as Christ's witness you can take good care of the planted seed by providing what it needs to grow. In 1 Corinthians 3:5–9, the things that you can do to nurture the seed that has been planted are referred to as "*watering.*"

How do we water as witnesses of Jesus? We nurture the Word of God with more of the Word of God. Two very effective ways that we can continue to share God's Word with people after we've first planted it—two ways to water the seed—are to invite them to things that will keep the conversation about Jesus going and to use God's Word to encourage them.

Water by Continuing the Conversation

Because you are Jesus' witness to the people in your everyday life, in most situations you will have opportunities to continue the conversation you are having. Sometimes those conversations will continue without any prompting on your part, but it's better to be intentional about continuing them by inviting the other person to something that will keep the conversation going.

Before you make an invitation, think about how the other person is going to receive it. The best invitations are those that are interesting and appealing from the other person's perspective. By this point in your conversation, it should be clear to you what that might be. You've listened to the other person and asked him questions. You've found a point of connection between his story and Jesus' story. You've observed and responded to his reaction to the Word that you've shared. The insight you've gained will help you extend an invitation that he will find interesting and appealing.

There are no standard invitations because invitations are relational and contextual. We need to craft them for an individual person to fit her unique circumstances. For example, after learning that a dechurched friend really misses the beauty of liturgical worship and being a part of a worshiping community, you might invite her to attend a worship service with you. On the other hand, if she had a very hurtful experience in her last congregation that led to her leaving the Church, you would not invite her to attend a worship service (or another church-based activity) as a starting point. Instead, you might invite her to talk about her hurtful experience over lunch or coffee.

In addition to considering what the other person would find interesting and appealing, you should consider the following factors when making an invitation to someone:

- The context of your relationship with the person
- The other person's response to what you've already shared
- What options and opportunities are available (and appropriate)
- The appearance (or the actuality) of a "bait-and-switch" invitation
- Who might be the best person to continue this conversation

Let's take a closer look at each of these factors by considering some guiding questions.

What is the context of your relationship with the other person?

Make sure that the invitation you want to make fits the context of your relationship with the person you are inviting. If you have been friends for several years, an invitation to come to your house for dinner and conversation would fit the relationship. But in our culture, the same invitation would probably not be a good invitation to extend to a new co-worker after having lunch together once or twice in your workplace. Coming to your home may feel too intimate to a person who doesn't know you well. A more fitting invitation would be to meet in a public place, such as a restaurant or coffee shop.

Another thing to keep in mind about the context of your relationship is whether or not you are physically located near each other. If you are engaging a person in a conversation through email or social media who lives in a distant community, inviting her to an activity or event in your community isn't going to be very effective. Digital and long-distance relationships will limit your options, but the fact that you are connected with the other person means that there are opportunities to invite him to continue the conversation within the context of your relationship.

How has the other person reacted to what you've shared so far?

Listening to how the other person has reacted to what you've already shared with him is an important key to understanding which invitations would interest and appeal to him and which ones are likely to be rejected. If his reaction has been one of interest and it seems as though he would like to hear more about God's Word, inviting him to come to a Bible study with you, recommending a daily devotion to read and discuss with you, or arranging a time to delve into the Word together could be an effective invitation. But you should avoid extending these same invitations if his reaction has indicated that he is not open to looking further into God's Word. Instead, you should invite him to something that would give you the opportunity to listen to more of his story and look for another opportunity to share Jesus' story with him.

What options and opportunities are available (and appropriate)?

There's an old saying that if the only solution you have is a hammer, then all your problems look like nails. In the same way, if the only option you have for inviting someone to something is your congregation's worship service, then you're going to invite everyone to worship. While that might be a good invitation in some contexts for some people, it is often an ineffective invitation for many people in many contexts.

It's important to think about what other options and opportunities exist for continuing your conversation about Jesus with a person.

Not only do we want to extend invitations that are of interest and are appealing to the other person, but we also want to make sure that the invitation is appropriate. For example, in most cases it wouldn't be appropriate for a married man to invite a single woman to have dinner with him at an elegant restaurant so the two of them can continue their conversation. And it is never appropriate to use "bait-and-switch" tactics when inviting someone to an event or activity.

Will the other person see this as a "bait-and-switch" invitation?

"Bait-and-switch" is when you invite someone to something that isn't what you say it is or it includes something that you don't tell the other person about. An example of "bait-and-switch" would be inviting your neighbor to an open gym night at your church's school to play volleyball, but when she shows up to play volleyball, you tell her, "Oh, before we start playing, we have a devotion and prayer with our pastor." While there's absolutely nothing wrong with having a devotion before open gym volleyball, your neighbor came to the event expecting only volleyball, based on your invitation. You may have gotten your neighbor to one devotion, but after duping her into participating in a devotion, she is unlikely to accept any future invitations from you. "Bait-and-switch" destroys trust. Make sure your invitations are complete.

If you don't fully know what you are inviting someone to, you may be involved in "bait-and-switch" unintentionally. I remember being invited by a co-worker to a concert at his church in which he had a prominent role. Several of the people I worked with came to the event at his invitation, including some nonchurched people. They came to support him and to enjoy a concert. At the end of the concert the pastor of the church addressed the audience. He said that the singing was nice, "but the real reason we're here tonight is to get right with God." He then proceeded to give a very pointed sermon to all the unsaved people in the audience and make a high-pressured altar call. I was embarrassed for my friend and uncomfortable for my nonchurched co-workers enduring this "bait-and-switch" tactic. Make sure you fully know what you are inviting people to.

Would another witness of Jesus be better able to continue this conversation?

There are times when the best invitation is one that includes other people. Sometimes it means that you aren't part of the invitation. This is especially true when you are likely to be unable to continue the conversation with someone. When you recognize that you may not be available to continue the conversation or that you may not be the best person to keep the conversation going, invite the person to connect with someone you know who would be a good person to continue it. Don't feel like you've dropped the ball or that you aren't a good witness when you do this. Witnessing is not a "me and Jesus" exercise that starts and ends with you. It involves the whole Body of Christ. Connecting a person to another witness of Jesus may be the best way for him to keep hearing the Word of God.

Watering Includes Following Up

Making an invitation isn't the end of watering as Christ's witness. Without proper follow-up, many invitations die on the vine. Even when a person accepts your invitation, it's important to follow up after the activity or event that he attended. Following up in a caring manner reinforces that you care about the other person as a person. It opens up new avenues for your conversation that provide you with opportunities to listen and ask and learn more about the other person.

Good follow-up shows the other person that you are interested and invested in her. It strengthens your relationship and increases trust. Following up well involves proper timing, respecting boundaries, and using appropriate methods.

Proper timing

Timing can make the difference between your actions being seen as encouraging or as pestering. Work to find the balance between becoming a nuisance by contacting the person too frequently and leaving the person wondering if you've forgotten about him because of letting too much time go by without contact. Timing is definitely more art than science. For example, a "Head" person may only want contact when there's a specific reason, but a "Heart" person may feel that you have forgotten about him or don't care about him if too much time passes between contacts.

Respecting boundaries

Following up effectively includes taking the proper approach with a person. This calls for understanding and following cultural and social norms. It also involves paying attention to appropriate boundaries. For example, it would be proper for a married man to send an encouraging email to a female neighbor to follow up on a conversation, but it would not be proper for him to send her a dozen roses to brighten up her day.

Using appropriate methods of following up

Tools are the resources that we can use to encourage people. Many different communication tools are available. The best tools are those with which the other person is most comfortable. A "Head" person might be very receptive to an email with a link to an article that is related to your last conversation, but that same person might be put off by a handwritten note to remind her that you've been thinking about her (which a "Heart" person would love!). A "Hands" person would appreciate receiving a copy of a newsletter that highlights a project that he worked on with you.

CHAPTER 8

HOW DO I WITNESS?—
WAITING EXPECTANTLY

And [Jesus] said, "The kingdom of God is
as if a man should scatter seed on the ground.
He sleeps and rises night and day, and the seed
sprouts and grows; he knows not how.
The earth produces by itself, first the blade,
then the ear, then the full grain in the ear. But
when the grain is ripe, at once he puts in the sickle,
because the harvest has come." Mark 4:26–29

Waiting Expectantly

We live in an era when everything happens quickly. Things that used to take a lot of time can now happen in a very short amount of time. As I'm writing this paragraph, I'm traveling from Florida to Texas by plane to celebrate my youngest granddaughter's first birthday. I left Ocala after worship services and a board meeting and will be in Dallas in time to have dinner with my family and watch Abby destroy her birthday cake. My wife and I will return to Florida in two days. It wasn't terribly long ago that a trip like this would have taken months by horse and wagon. People marveled when trains shortened the time to days. Now we are used to these kinds of trips taking only hours.

Travel isn't the only part of our lives that has sped up. Email has all but replaced mailing letters. Checks that once took days to clear are now processed instantly. Waiting for the next episode in a television series has given way to binge-watching one episode after another. It used to be that a mail-order item took four to six weeks to be delivered. Now, we expect the item we order on the Internet to be delivered in two days—and if we live in an urban area, it might be delivered in a few hours. We've never been very good at waiting. Now we don't need to wait in many aspects of our lives.

But there are some things that still take time. Babies still grow in the womb for nine months. Holidays, birthdays, and anniversaries are still once-a-year events. The seasons move at the same pace that they have for thousands of years. As any farmer knows, it takes time for the seed that is sown in the soil to germinate, grow, and mature. There's nothing that the farmer can do to speed up this process. He must wait for the harvest.

Jesus used the image of a farmer waiting for the harvest to explain what the kingdom of God is like. It was an example from everyday life for the people who first heard Him teach. It has stood the test of time very well. Even people like us who rush through life with ever-increasing expectations of things becoming more instantaneous realize that going from seed to harvest takes time. It means waiting. Waiting is something we do not value. Most of us see waiting as a waste of valuable time. But waiting is an important part of being Christ's witnesses. The waiting we're called to do between sowing and harvesting is waiting with a purpose.

The purpose of waiting as witnesses of Jesus is found in the parable that He used to describe the Kingdom. He explained that after the farmer sowed his seed, he did not know how the seed sprouted and grew. That doesn't sound like he was much of a farmer, does it? Today's farmers can explain in great detail the scientific process by which seeds germinate and mature into fruitful plants. But today's farmers also know that the seed will never sprout if the right conditions don't develop. They are as dependent as the farmer in Jesus' parable on the Lord to craft those conditions and cause the seed to grow.

This is what waiting in witnessing is all about. As Christ's witness, you can sow the seeds of His Word, but you can't cause them to sprout and grow. You know that witnessing is a process of plowing, sowing, and watering, but you don't know what God will do with the seeds you plant. You don't know who will come to faith. You don't know when a person might come to faith. There is a lot that you don't know, but there's one thing that I want you to know about being Jesus' witness: your waiting is not in vain.

God has given us a beautiful promise regarding the seeds of His Word that we sow: "As the rain and the snow come down from heaven and do not return there but water the earth, making it bring forth and sprout, giving seed to the sower and bread to the eater, so shall My word be that goes out from My mouth; it shall not return to Me empty, but it shall accomplish that which I purpose, and shall succeed in the thing for which I sent it" (Isaiah 55:10–11).

Based on this promise, we can be comfortable with not knowing a lot of things, and we can be confident that God's Word will accomplish what He desires. Like a farmer who can wait because he knows that the harvest is coming, we can wait in joyful expectation that God will gather all of His elect into His kingdom. That harvest is certain to come. As a faithful witness of Jesus, you can wait expectantly.

Waiting Actively

There's another dimension to waiting that we don't want to overlook. That dimension is that waiting for the harvest is active, not passive. There is a lot of work to do while we are waiting. In the parable, Jesus emphasizes this by saying, "He sleeps and rises night and day" as the process of sprouting and growing happens without the farmer knowing how. But not knowing *how* doesn't mean the farmer didn't know *what*. In his "rising" each day, he labors in his fields to do what he can to aid the plants in their growth. His days are filled with weeding, pest control, and fertilizing. The work of nurturing doesn't stop as we wait for the harvest.

After my grandfather retired from working as a carpenter, he bought a fifteen-acre farm in West Brooklyn, Ill. He had been raised on a farm, and it was his lifelong dream to return to living on a farm. He had an amazing gift for growing things. His little farm produced a variety of food, including potatoes, peppers, green beans, peas, sweet corn that tasted like manna from heaven, and red, juicy tomatoes that shamed the grocery store's anemic offerings. He loved to sell what he grew at his roadside stand, where he became locally well-known for the many stories he "sold" along with his vegetables. Since we lived only an hour away, I was able to visit the farm frequently, and I got to spend time on the farm during the summer months. I was usually there for summer stays after the seeds were sown and before the bulk of the harvest. Whenever I stayed on the farm, I was put to work, so I know firsthand that waiting for the harvest is active.

One summer I was at the farm when the onions were sprouting. My grandfather put me to work weeding the onions to help them grow better. He sat me down next to a row of onions that was about four miles long, pointed out what an onion sprout looked like, and we got busy. He weeded his row at three times my speed as I fumbled with determining which plants were weeds and which were onion sprouts. I'm sure that the onion harvest from my row was a little disappointing that year.

My experience weeding onions illustrates what it looks like to actively wait for the harvest as a witness of Jesus. After planting the seeds and nurturing the soil by listening to a person, asking good questions to better understand her, finding a way of sharing Jesus' story with her in a way that she can hear and relate to, and encouraging her to keep the conversation going, we still have work to do as we wait to see if or when the Holy Spirit is going to produce fruit in her. We can be certain that between the sowing of the seed of God's Word and the harvest that comes when a person believes His Word, Satan will be at work to destroy what has been planted. We know this because Jesus made it clear in another agricultural parable, which is found in Matthew 13:

> [Jesus] put another parable before them, saying, "The kingdom of heaven may be compared to a man who sowed good seed in his field, but while his men were sleeping, his enemy came and sowed weeds among the wheat and went away. So when the plants came up and bore grain, then the weeds appeared also. And

the servants of the master of the house came and said to him, 'Master, did you not sow good seed in your field? How then does it have weeds?' He said to them, 'An enemy has done this.' So the servants said to him, 'Then do you want us to go and gather them?' But he said, 'No, lest in gathering the weeds you root up the wheat along with them. Let both grow together until the harvest, and at harvest time I will tell the reapers, "Gather the weeds first and bind them in bundles to be burned, but gather the wheat into my barn."'" (Matthew 13:24–30)

After Jesus told this parable, His disciples asked Him to explain it to them. He explained, "The one who sows the good seed is the Son of Man. The field is the world, and the good seed is the sons of the kingdom. The weeds are the sons of the evil one, and the enemy who sowed them is the devil. The harvest is the end of the age, and the reapers are angels" (Matthew 13:37–39). As we apply this parable to our lives as Christ's witnesses, we want to be faithful to Jesus' explanation of it. The parable makes three things clear to us as we go about the work of witnessing: Satan is actively working to undermine God's kingdom work; there will be a harvest of people who by grace through faith will receive eternal life; and there will be a gathering for condemnation of the people who do not have faith in Jesus. These realities create a sense of urgent waiting for us.

Waiting Urgently

We know that there is going to be a final harvest and people who do not belong to Jesus will be separated from Him forever. But we don't know when that harvest is going to take place. If the harvest is decades away, we can be patient and wait comfortably. However, if it is days away, we need to do something right now.

Jesus had some things to say about the timing of the harvest. Regarding the end of time and the final harvest, He told His disciples that "concerning that day and hour no one knows, not even the angels of heaven, nor the Son, but the Father only" (Matthew 24:36). But He also wanted them (and us) to understand that the harvest is taking place every day as we wait for it to be completed. He pointed them to the Samaritans streaming from the town of Sychar to hear His teachings and told the disciples, "Do you not say, 'There are yet four months, then comes the harvest'? Look, I tell you, lift up your eyes, and see that the fields are white for harvest" (John 4:35).

The harvest is coming, but the harvest is also now. It is never far off. It is always near. Because of that, we sense the need to do something to make things happen rather than wait on the Lord to act in His time. However, like the servants in the parable of the weeds and the wheat, we don't know which people are "weeds" and which people are "wheat."

Like my destructive onion weeding experience, we're just as likely to uproot someone who will come to faith and bear fruit as we are to dismiss a person as unbelieving. My grandfather expertly distinguished between an onion sprout and a weed. Only God can distinguish between people who will come to faith before the harvest and people who will perish in their sins.

So what are we to do as Christ's witnesses as we urgently, actively, and expectantly wait for the harvest that will finally reveal who is wheat and who is weeds? Acting on our understanding that the harvest is not a single event at the end of time, we plow and plant and nurture in the many different fields God calls us to through our various relationships. And we do so in confidence that the harvest—individually or collectively—is at hand.

CHAPTER 9

HOW DO I WITNESS?—HARVESTING

Other seeds fell on good soil and produced grain, some a hundredfold, some sixty, some thirty. Matthew 13:8

One of my favorite Bible verses about witnessing doesn't seem to have much to do with witnessing at first glance. But the picture that it paints is one that describes the day when the harvest will be more plentiful than ever before. "'Behold, the days are coming,' declares the LORD, 'when the plowman shall overtake the reaper and the treader of grapes him who sows the seed; the mountains shall drip sweet wine, and all the hills shall flow with it'" (Amos 9:13). What a beautiful thought. The demanding work of plowing, planting, nurturing, and waiting will be eclipsed by the joyful work of harvesting.

Jesus alluded to Amos 9:13 when He was speaking to His disciples outside of the Samaritan town of Sychar after

His conversation with a woman of poor reputation from that village. In addition to telling them that the fields were white with harvest, Jesus said to His disciples, "Already the one who reaps is receiving wages and gathering fruit for eternal life, so that sower and reaper may rejoice together. For here the saying holds true, 'One sows and another reaps.' I sent you to reap that for which you did not labor. Others have labored, and you have entered into their labor" (John 4:36–38).

Jesus was telling His disciples that He had chosen to give them the work of harvesting. Other people were given the work of plowing, planting, and nurturing. Their work was necessary for there to be a harvest. Although other people had to do their work without seeing the harvest, they were not bitter, angry, or disappointed about the work that they had been given to do. They rejoiced and were glad in view of the harvest that they knew by faith would eventually come. They knew that others would reap from what they had sown, and that gave them joy. As Jesus said, "Sower and reaper may rejoice together."

Who will reap what you sow as a witness of Jesus? When will the harvest take place? Will you see any of the harvest? There's no way of knowing the answers to these questions with certainty. As Amos 9:13 pictures things, you may well be involved in both planting and harvesting. On the other hand, you may spend a lifetime sowing seeds and not see the harvest—that is, not see the harvest in this life.

Whatever happens, you can be sure that the seeds of God's Word will accomplish what He purposes for them and that some will produce fruit: "some a hundredfold, some sixty, some thirty" (Matthew 13:8). And you can be certain that you will see the harvest on the Last Day.

Do Not Grow Weary

Being members of a results-oriented culture, we may get discouraged when we don't see the results that we hope for as witnesses of Jesus. Most of us would much rather be harvesters than plowers and planters. My favorite time to be at my grandparents' farm was when crops were ripening and we were gathering in the fruit that came from my grandfather's hard work. I definitely enjoyed picking tomatoes (with a salt shaker in my back pocket) more than I did weeding that four-mile-long row of onions.

In much the same way, I would rather be working with people as they come to faith, profess Jesus, and are received into His family through Holy Baptism than I would be plowing the hard soil of people who are ignorant of, opposed to, indifferent toward, or confused about spiritual matters. Yet I know that there can't be a harvest unless someone has sown and nurtured the seeds. I also know that it is not up to me whether I am a sower or a reaper. The Lord has chosen the roles that He has designed for His witnesses according to His plan and purposes.

Remembering the picture painted in Amos 9:13 and Jesus' proclamation that a day is coming when the reaper and the sower will rejoice together helps to keep things in perspective. The encouragement of Galatians 6:9, "And let us not grow weary of doing good, for in due season we will reap, if we do not give up," should certainly bolster us as Christ's witnesses. But sometimes we could use a little more. Sometimes we need a glimpse of the harvest.

A Glimpse of the Harvest

I vividly remember a time when God granted me a glimpse of the harvest. After coming back to the Church as a young man, I was very enthusiastic about witnessing. I spoke about the faith whenever I had an opportunity, including in my workplace. I was working for the Motorola Corporation when I decided to enroll in the seminary. This didn't surprise my co-workers, but it did trouble one of them. Keith was not a Christian, and he couldn't understand why I would give up the opportunities I had for a good career with Motorola to go into the ministry. I don't know why he was so concerned and so adamant, but he took it upon himself to convince me not to leave Motorola. I used his nearly daily visits to my cubicle to tell him about Jesus.

As things turned out, after my first year at the seminary, I faced a major crisis. My very troubled wife had an affair and left me and our daughter, who was not quite two years old. Reeling from this disaster, hoping to salvage our marriage, and suddenly dealing with being a single father, I left the seminary and moved back to Arizona. I was unemployed for a number of months. Things were getting desperate. I was despondent as I experienced what has been called "the dark night of the soul."

My situation began to turn around. I was rehired by Motorola and started getting my new life in order. Things were hard, but things were looking up. Then one day at lunchtime, I saw Keith across the cafeteria at Motorola—or, I should say, Keith saw me. He not only saw me, he was calling out my name. As he made his way toward me, I looked down and said under my breath, "Thanks, Lord. Just what I needed." I knew what was coming. Keith had tried to convince me to forget about the seminary and to pursue a career with Motorola. I knew a big "I told you so" was coming.

But Keith was coming toward me with a huge smile on his face. He was so excited to see me. He said, "I heard you were back, and I was hoping to see you. I wanted to thank you for all the time you spent with me before you went to the seminary. I didn't understand what you were talking about then, but while you were gone, I became a Christian. Thank you for sharing God's Word with me." As Keith walked away, I looked up and said, "Thanks, Lord. Just what I needed."

The Lord had blessed me with a glimpse of the harvest just when I needed it most.

Joy Is Set before You

I don't know if the Lord will ever give you a glimpse of the harvest. And I don't know if He has called you to sow or to reap or to do a bit of both. But I do know that He is calling you to share in His joy over the harvest wherever and whenever He gathers people into His Church. He has given you a part in the work that is near and dear to His heart—the work that brings Him joy.

The joy of the harvest is pictured beautifully by Jesus in a series of parables found in Luke 15. In the first parable He talks about one out of a hundred sheep that goes missing (i.e., is lost). Then He tells a parable about a woman who looks for the one coin missing from her stash of ten coins. In the third parable, Jesus speaks about one of two sons who is lost to his father when he takes his inheritance and goes away. In each of these parables something (or someone) is lost. And in each of these parables there is great joy when what was lost is found. "Rejoice with me" is the refrain of the one who finds what was lost. The finder is so filled with joy that he or she wants to share that joy with others.

You have been given a tremendous privilege. God has called you to be His witness and to join Him in His mission to "seek and to save the lost" (Luke 19:10). In calling you to be His witness, Jesus is also calling you to share in His joy. "Rejoice with Me" is His invitation to all who answer His call to bring the Good News to those who are lost. You may not see much of the harvest in this life. You may experience more hardship and disappointment than joy in your labors as you plow, plant, nurture, and wait expectantly.

But a day is coming when you will rejoice with Jesus as you gather around His throne with thousands upon thousands and ten thousands upon ten thousands of people who were once lost but who have been found by the grace of God. There you will be in the full presence of the Lord with neighbors, family members, co-workers, teammates, classmates, and all kinds of people who were part of your everyday life—some of whom will be there because you were the witness the Holy Spirit used to bring the Word of life to them.

Until that day, you can labor with confidence in the plowing, planting, nurturing, expectant waiting, and harvesting of witnessing. This is the calling God has on your life. This is your purpose for being in the world. Joy is set before you. "Rejoice with Me!" Jesus is calling out above the noise of the world and the fears of your heart. "Come, My faithful witness, share in My joy!"